Table of Contents

Tools Of The Trade

TOOLS

The **stylus** tools and Teflon tip tools, are used to create the impression.

The **refiners** will sharpen the edge of the impression.

The **detailer** tool is used for adding fine lines to the impression.

The **cutting** tool is used on a cutting mat to cut the edges of the metal, and useful for opening in the center of the design embossed in metal.

ERASERS

There are three sizes of **erasers** with five different tips. Erasers are also used as stylus tools for creating an impression and can be used as refiners. They are also used to smooth out and remove impression mistakes in all types of metal.

SURFACES

All of the tools listed here work the best on a smooth or foam surface.

The **acrylic mat** is a must for providing a smooth surface to refine or erase mistakes. The **thick foam mat**, gives the **Ball & Cups** a deeper impression, while the *thin foam mat* is great for using with **Decorative Wheels** and embossing.

Embossed Metal Sample

Patterned Molds

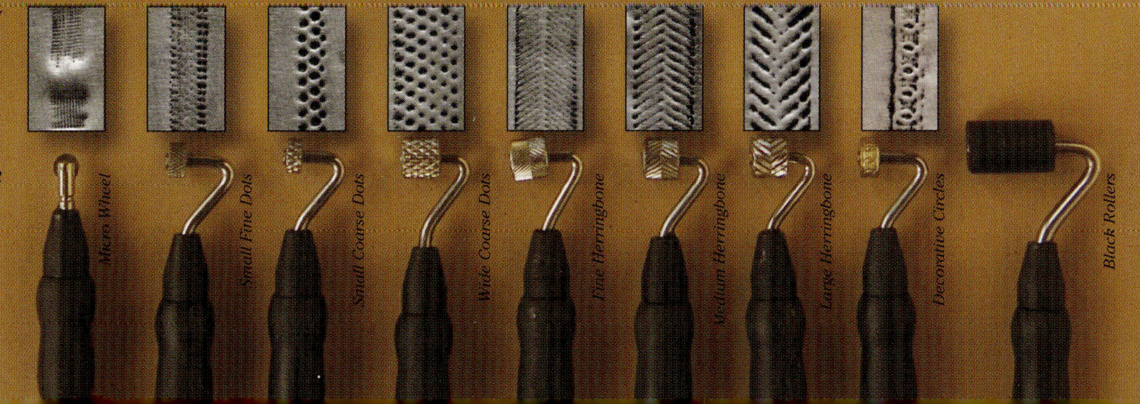

Ball & Cups

Humungo

Large

Medium

Small

Large Brass Brush

Paper Stump

MOLDS

Repetitive metal embossing is a snap with patterned *Molds.*

Molds can be used with polymer clay, PMC, fun foam, and pencil rubbings.

BALL & CUPS

Create dimensional dome shapes with ease. *Paper Stumps* are used to puff and smooth out metal.

Add dimension quickly with *Decorative Wheels* by rolling out impressions in metal, clay or cardstock. Smooth and define designs with the *Black Roller*. For a brushed metal finish use the *Brass Brush* in a circular motion.

Metals

Shown here are the various metals that are used in Metal Effects. They are brass, aluminum, copper, pewter, art metal foils, metal tape and decorative foiling tape for stained glass.

Metal thickness is measured by gauge. The lower the number gauge, the thicker the metal. The optimum embossing gauge is 36-38. All of the metals used in this book were in this range.

Art metals are a light gauge aluminum with a color coating on one side. They are generally on the thinner side and can be as thin as paper. The coating on these metals can be sanded off, which can create a unique look after it's been embossed. Metal tape and copper or silver soldering tapes have an adhesive on one side and can be decorated with the wheels and other tools shown on page 4.

Pewter and tin have a warmer color to them than aluminum, and are softer to use than the other metals. However, they contain Lead, so care should be taken when working with them. Wash hands thoroughly, before and after working with metals. Never eat and emboss at the same time.

Supplies

Most of the supplies shown here have been used throughout this book and should be a part of your basic supply kit:

Stencils

Decorative Punches

Acrylic Paints

Non-Porous Ink Pads

The Ultimate Adhesive

Lightweight Spackle

Paintbrushes

Wax Paper

Scissors

Rubber Stamps

Paper Towels

Let's Talk Design

If you happen to have the ability to free hand a design or letter a poem, fantastic! Designs can also be created using stencils, rubber stamps, computer-generated art or lettering, and clip art books. Almost any drawing, sketch or photo can be translated into metal. I suggest starting out with a simple line drawing with minimal detail until you get used to the tools.

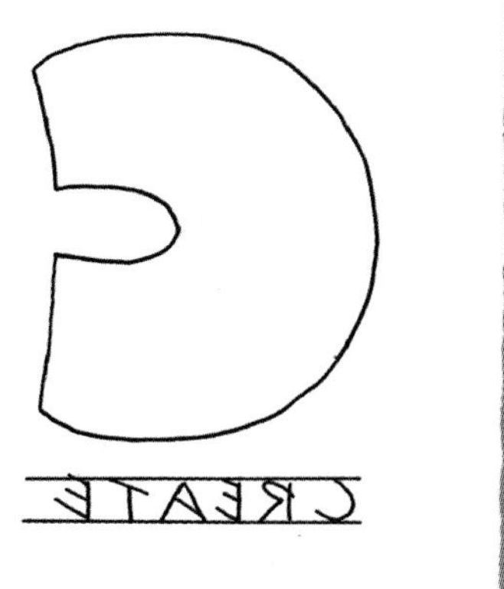

The letter shown was drawn from a Deja View template. "Create" was hand-lettered within a 1/4" border.

Copy or print a mirror image of designs that are lettering. This will read backwards and enable you to emboss your lettering. Any lettering seen in this book with an embossed look was created with a mirror image.

About © Copyright
Not wanting to go into legal detail on such issues, I will say that it is crucial that any design that you embark upon reproducing be copyright free. Laws vary greatly, so do your homework, especially if you plan to sell a piece.

TIPS

❖ *If a smaller or larger design is needed, simply change the size on a copier.*

❖ *Dig out all those templates, rubber stamps and stencils in your drawers and give them new life with Metal Effects.*

❖ *It is best to copy the designs on vellum when possible. Vellum can withstand the pressure of your stylus several times.*

Let's Get Started

Cheryl Darrow, Designer

To get started, your basic tool kit for metal embossing should include:

Teflon & Stylus tool	Cutting Mat
Refiner	Acrylic Mat
Cutter	Foam Mats - Thick and Thin
Various Decorative Wheels	Acrylic Paint
Various Ball & Cups	Crafter's Pick The Ultimate! Glue
Paper Stump	Craft Tape Sheets
Black Roller	Lightweight Spackle
Scissors	1" Paintbrush
Round Dowel	Various templates, patterns or
Wax Paper	computer generated text

Note: *There is no right or wrong side to your design unless you are embossing words. You must decide which look you want on the front, either Embossed or Debossed. It's all a judgment call, so if you want your design to have a heavy antiqued look, then most of the design will be worked on top. (Debossed image)*

(Top side) **Embossed Line**   (Top side) **Debossed Line**

Place a piece of metal, cut larger than the design on acrylic mat and flatten with the black roller tool.

Tape design to the metal and place on top of thin foam mat. When working on the foam mat, always have the acrylic mat under it. Using the Teflon tip tool, trace the pattern and word on the metal.

Now to refine the design. Flip the metal over to the front, remove foam mat and using the refiner tool, run it along the outside edge only of the design. This will create a crisp line on the outside of the design.

Metal Effects

Embellishing

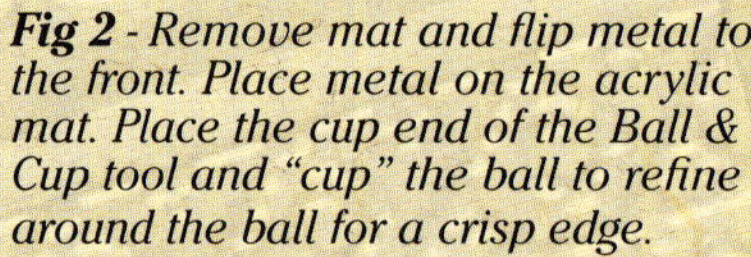

Divide up the letter into sections and start the design. Use a grid design and this will give a nice embossed edge on the front of the metal.

Fig 1 - Use the ball end of the Ball & Cup to create "balls" on the design. The thick mat must be used under the metal.

Fig 2 - Remove mat and flip metal to the front. Place metal on the acrylic mat. Place the cup end of the Ball & Cup tool and "cup" the ball to refine around the ball for a crisp edge.

Fill in sections using the Teflon tip tool and create doodles, squiggles or swirls.

Using the micro wheel, fill in the grid on the front with super fine lines.

Refine around each letter and the border. Use the Teflon tip tool to refine around small spaces in lettering. For an added finish, decorate the edge of the metal with any of the decorative wheels.

For extra texture use the brass brush in a circular motion and give the metal a brushed finish.

Metal Effects

Puffing

To create a "puffed" look, flip the metal over and hold it in the palm of your hand. Gently rub the inside of the design with the end of the paper stump in the area that is to be puffed. You will see the metal stretch.

Turn the metal over to the front and place on the acrylic mat. Use the paper stump and trace around the edges of the metal. This will make the puffed design stand out. You may need to puff the backside several times and refine the top until you have the desired effect.

Run the black roller around the letter to flatten around the design.

Using Spackle, fill in the design on the back. I usually use my finger for this, or the end of the black roller. This must be filled so that it won't flatten under pressure.

*Place a piece of wax paper over the Spackle and rub with the paper stump. This will take out air bubbles and compact the Spackle. *Fill in any area that you don't want flattened.*

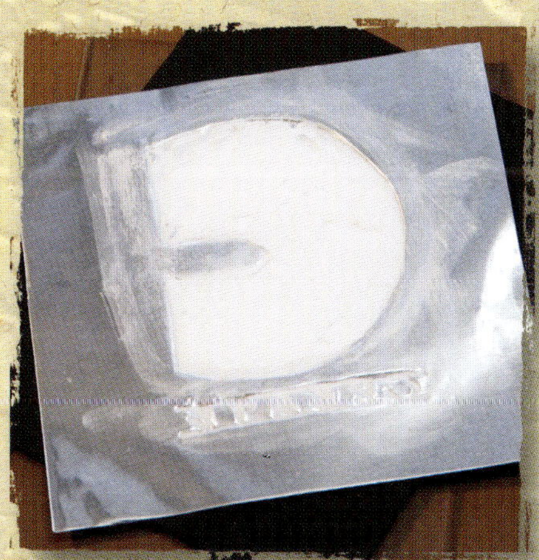

Wipe off excess around the design and let dry until hardened.

Metal Effects

Antiquing & Gluing

There are many antiquing finishes that can be used on metal. Several will give aluminum and copper a beautiful verdigris or rusted finish. Most of the projects shown in this book were done using acrylic paints. Experiment with different products to achieve the finish you desire.

TIP
Create a shabby-chic look by painting the metal and lightly sanding the top so the metal comes through.

Apply acrylic paint with a brush, pushing the paint into all the crevices.

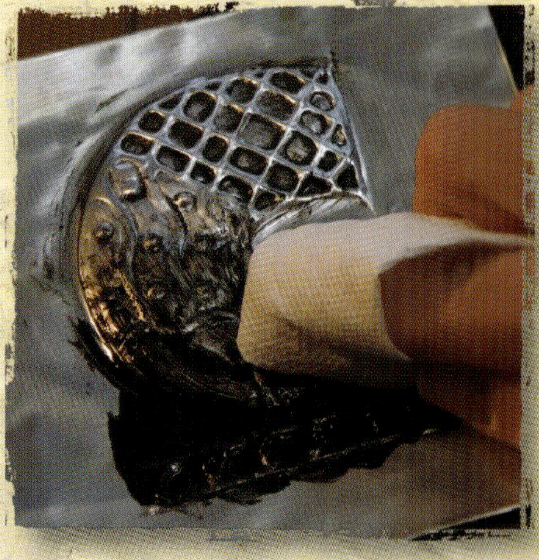

Wipe off excess with a paper towel and let dry.

Several types of adhesive can be used in the mounting process. Craft tape in sheet form is the least messy. Peel off the backing of the sheets.

  Metal Effects

Place on metal and peel off outer layer of craft tape sheets. Then mount on cardstock or any surface. Remember these tape sheets are sticky and very hard to undo. Once it's placed on something it's there forever.

The Ultimate! Glue is a great alternative adhesive for use on metal. Paint on a thin but even layer and then apply to any surface. This will take about 20 minutes to dry, but gives you time to adjust placement if needed.

Uh-Oh!
How Do I Fix This?

So what do you do when you mess up? Throw it away, start over or vow you'll never touch metal again! Well, you could do those things but I like to fix my mess-ups. It's so simple, you'll never throw away any metal.

TIPS

❖ *Repair tears in the metal with metal tape which is silver on both sides. Press the metal tape into the groove of the tear on the backside.*

❖ *Squiggles around the letters as a background or detail lines made with a detailer can also hide mistakes.*

First, you need to know your tools. You've probably noticed the tools with white tips in various shapes and sizes. They are erasers, but they do more than just erase.

In figure 1, the word happy is misspelled.

Using the flat edge of the large chiseled tip eraser, shown in figure 2, flatten the mistake on both sides of the metal.

Always erase on the acrylic mat. Since I want the letter to be a "P", there is no need to erase the whole letter.

The mistake is still visible on the metal but that space is now smooth.

Fill in the part of the letter that is being changed on a foam mat and refine around the edges on the acrylic mat.

The part of the letter than can still be seen just needs to be hidden. For a brushed metal look, a brass brush gives a nice finish.

Metal Effects

Stamping On Metal

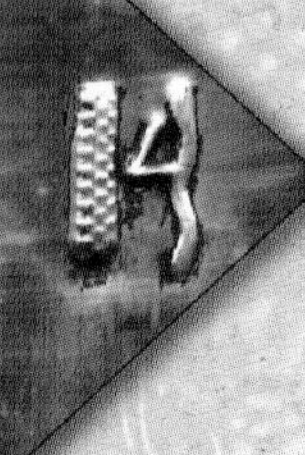

Use an ink pad for non-porous surfaces. Stamp on the back of the metal. Let dry.

Place metal on a foam mat and trace image with a stylus or Teflon embossing tool.

Flip the metal over and refine the design on the acrylic mat. For another look, images could be stamped on the front of the metal and, using the Teflon tool, accent just certain parts of the design.

Metal Effects

MISCELLANEOUS TIPS

❖ *Use a 2 lb. sack of rice to place on top of pieces as they are drying in the gluing stage. The rice will mold to the shape of the project and not squash the design.*

❖ *Never store tools and metal in the same containers or they will rust!*

❖ *Pewter contains LEAD. Never heat it. Never eat while handling any of the metals and take care to wash hands thoroughly before eating.*

❖ *Don't let rules keep you from trying various other techniques, antiquing processes or creating your own look with Metal Effects. As with any craft, the most fun comes from experimenting.*

Projects
15

Aspire To Be

Cheryl Darrow, Designer,
Figure 1

This project uses wood letters and other ephemera found around the house. I've created these inside cigar boxes or for a very impressive look on mat-board and framed.

Supplies Used:
Wood Letter 5" (Twelve Timbers)
Aluminum 6" x 6"
Acrylic Paint: Yellow, Red, Black
Foam Brush
Canvas Board
Bottle Caps
Stickers
Background Stamps: PostModern Designs
Black Memory Ink: Colorbox
Painter's Tape
Craft Knife
Decorative Wheels
Ball & Cups
Teflon Embossing Tool
E-6000 Adhesive
Crafter's Pick The Ultimate! Glue
Alphabet Letter Tiles
Cutting Mat

*****S**hown here are various tools, metal and a painted wooden letter. In figure 1, metal is used only on the face of the letter A.*

Place metal on top of letter and, using the black roller, impress the outline of the letter. This will give you the outline in the best detail.

Metal Effects

Place metal on foam mat and emboss design of your choice. Antique the metal and let dry. (See basic embossing and antiquing instructions).

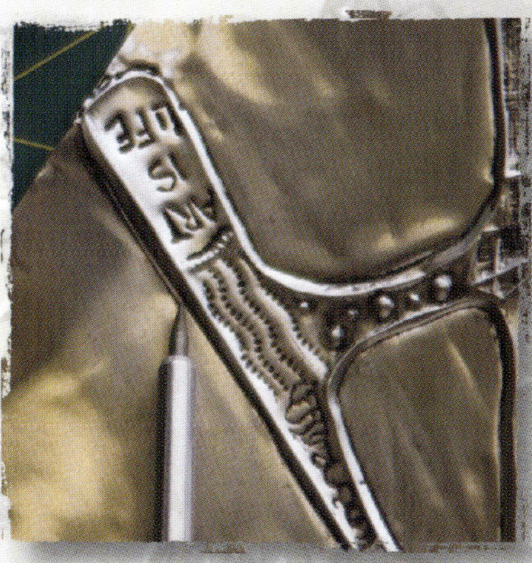

Place metal on a cutting mat. Using the cutting tool, cut out the "A" along the edge of the embossed design.

Apply The Ultimate Glue to the top of the wooden letter.

Place cut out of metal letter on the wood. (Weigh down with a bag of rice and let dry). The completed letter is glued on the canvas board using E-6000 adhesive.

Paint canvas board with acrylic paints and let dry. Mask off a grid pattern with painter's tape. (I tore the tape for a deckle edge) Apply black acrylic paint to the center of this grid and let dry. At this point the background can be stamped and collaged as shown in Fig. 1.

Bend back bottle cap edge with heavy pliers. Paint insides with black acrylic paint. Glue alphabet tiles in the center of cap with The Ultimate Glue. These are then glued on the canvas board with E-6000. (Bottle caps make great frames for alphabet tiles.)

TIP: *Why not make your own alphabet tiles with metal. You will never run out of a letter!*

Metal Effects

Cigar Box

I love cigar boxes and all the wonderful graphics that are printed on them. This project uses the background of the box as part of the design.

Supplies Used:

Cigar Box
Metal Hooks (Home Improvement Store)
Handle (Home Improvement Store)
Aluminum to cover box on all sides
Black Acrylic Paint
Craft tape (in sheet form)
Drill and Drill Bit (to fit handle hole)
E-6000
Lightweight Spackle
Ball & Cup tool
Teflon Embossing Tool
Refiner
Black Roller

Cheryl Darrow, Designer

Above: Tools and materials needed for this project. Cut metal to fit all sides. Free form designs were embossed, debossed and antiqued on this cigar box.

Emboss and refine metal with Teflon embossing tool. A Ball & Cup tool was used to create this side panel design.

Use Spackle to fill in design. This helps to hold the shape of the words.

Metal Effects

Cut craft tape sheets to the same size as the embossed and antiqued metal. Peel off backing of the craft tape sheet and stick to the back of the finished metal. Caution: This adhesive is very strong and cannot be repositioned.

Carefully align and adhere embossed metal panel to the box.

Use black roller to smooth edges securely to the box.

Glue hooks in place using E-6000 adhesive. Let dry overnight.

Drill two holes for handle in the lid of the cigar box. Screw in handle. Use extra spacers if needed for the screws to fit in the handle.

TIPS

❖ *Patterns for quilt or stained glass projects can also be used.*

❖ *Wood blocks or game pieces can also be used as legs.*

Metal Effects

Decorative Plaque

Cheryl Darrow, Designer

I have a notebook of quotes that I collect. These can be hand-lettered or typeset in your favorite font. Just remember to create a mirror image copy for embossing.

Supplies Used:
Aluminum
Metal Tape
Medium Round Tip Eraser tool
Various Decorative Wheels
Ball & Cup
Craft Knife
Wooden Wreath form (craft store)
Round plastic decorative plate
Drill & Drill bit
Wire
Needle Nose pliers
Black Acrylic Paint
Pattern with saying

TIPS
Glass beads can be added to this step for another look.

Plaque can be hung on the wall or on a plate rack.

Tape reversed pattern to the back of the metal for the quotation. See basic instructions.

Use the medium round eraser tool to emboss the saying on the metal. Add Ball & Cup around lettering. Antique the metal.

Metal Effects

TIPS

❖ *Use medium gauge wire to fasten the wooden form and plate together.*

❖ *Substitute the saying with a photograph or a collage.*

Emboss and deboss abstract images using wheels and the medium point Eraser tool on the metal tape. Antique the tape and let dry. Cut the tape into lengths that will fit around the wooden wreath form.

Lay pre-drilled wooden form on top of decorative plastic plate.

Use wooden form as drilling template. I selected four holes to drill through the plastic plate for wiring forms together. Note: All holes may be used if desired.

Remove backing from tape and adhere to the wreath form. Overlap lengths of tape to create a crazy quilt effect on the wooden form. Glue the wooden form on top of the quotation.

Line up drilled holes and thread wire to come out to the front of the plaque. Using needle nose pliers, wrap the wire into a spiral and squish.

Metal Effects

Anniversary Card

Karen Wells, Designer

Molds are so easy to use and make embossing metal a snap.

Supplies Used
Aluminum 6" x 6"
Copper
Burgundy cardstock
Acrylic Paint: Ivory, Tan, and Black
Paintbrush
Crafter's Pick The Ultimate! Glue
Molds: #4; #20 and #41: Ten Seconds Studio
Paper Stump
Small Pointed Eraser

TIP
Experiment with paint color combinations and then lightly sand the tops of the embossed metal for a different effect.

Molds come with embossed or debossed designs. Either side of the metal can be used after it's been worked on the mold. The metal should be filled with Spackle to keep the designs in the metal from being crushed.

Metal Effects

Place metal on top of mold and rub with a paper stump. This will bring out the design. Tape the metal to the mold if needed.

Using the pointed Eraser, outline around the design to refine the image.

Mini Scrapbook

Antiquicize your very own one-of-a-kind *Metal Effects* mini scrapbook album with this painting technique.

Supplies Used:
Aluminum 6" x 6"
Copper
Copper Wire: Artistic Wire
Black Grommets & Copper Brads: Making Memories
Black Matboard
Black and Brown Cardstock
Ruler
Brush
Hole Punch
Acrylic Paint: Ivory, Tan and Black
Teflon Embossing Tool
Paper Stump
Ball & Cup
Mold #8: Ten Seconds Studio

Karen Wells, Designer

*E**mboss metal with mold #8 on four sides. Using a ruler, draw double lines with Teflon Embossing tool to create border.*

Refine lines. Use a Ball & Cup to create a ball border.

Paint the metal with ivory acrylic paint and let dry.

Dry brush tan acrylic paint over the top for an antique look.

Metal Effects

Imagine Card

Ball & Cup tools are so versatile when debossed or embossed on metal. Use decorative scissors for edging the designs.

Supplies Used:
Paper: Design Originals
Stamps: PostModern Design, PSX
Copper
Black Dye Inkpad: Clearsnap
Green and Gold Cardstock
Black Acrylic Paint
Lightweight Spackle
Decorative Scissors: Family Treasures
Craft Tape
Ribbon
Teflon Embossing Tool
Various Ball & Cups
Decorative Wheel

Karen Wells, Designer

Stamp image on aluminum and emboss with stylus tool.

Use two different sizes of Ball & Cups to add balls to the center of heart, flip over and cup the balls. Use the small Ball & Cup tool and deboss the ball pattern around heart. Do not cup the ball.

Puff the center of the hearts. Add Spackle and antique with acrylic paint. Trim with decorative scissors. Adhere to card. Debo "Imagine" with alphabet stamps on copp strip. Border with a decorative wheel.

Metal Effects

Happy Holidays Card

Karen Wells, Designer

Make this extra special and turn the embossed metal into an ornament attached to the card. In this project the image was stamped on the back of copper, and embossed. For another effect, stamp on the front of the metal with ink for non-porous surfaces and just emboss certain areas of the image.

Supplies Used:
Copper 2" x 2"
Copper tinted paper
Green Cardstock
Stamp: DeNami Design
Archival Black Inkpad: Clearsnap
Black Acrylic Paint
Paintbrush
Crafter's Pick The Ultimate! Glue
Teflon Embossing Tool
Decorative Wheels
Ball & Cups

Stamp design on back of copper with black ink.

Emboss and refine the design with the Teflon Embossing tool.

Section off copper and letter saying, then antique with acrylic paint. Asymmetrical embossed lines add to the design.

Metal Effects

Ten Seconds Sampler

Cheryl Darrow, Designer

This sampler will turn any altered book or album into a cherished keepsake. Why not frame it?

Supplies needed:
Pewter 6" x 6"
Teflon Embossing Tool
Various Ball & Cups
Various Decorative Wheels
Brass Brush
Black Acrylic Paint
1" Paintbrush
Metal-edged Ruler

TIP
Use design patterns from quilting or stained glass books.

Create a design on grid paper. Tape design to metal and place on foam mat. Trace pattern on metal with Teflon embossing tool and ruler.

Metal Effects

Create designs in the metal. Some of these are doodles and squiggles.

Refine all grid lines after the designs are embossed or debossed.

Metal Notebook

Angie Vangalis, Designer

Looking for a fast and creative gift? Turn a store-bought spiral notebook into an object de art! Beads and charms can be added for extra sparkle.

Supplies Used:
Small Spiral notebook
Metal Tape
Teflon Embossing Tool
Various Decorative Wheels
Fibers
Metal Tag
Black Acrylic Paint

*U*sing the embossing tool, deboss designs across a length of metal tape. Use decorative wheels to finish filling in the tape. Antique with acrylic paint.

Remove backing from tape and adhere to the front and back of a spiral notebook.

Finish layering metal tape and trim off the excess. Decorate with fibers or ribbon. A store-bought metal tag was also embossed. You can make your own metal tags in various sizes.

Metal Effects

Puffed & Mounted Letter

Turn old cigar box lids into special keepsake plaques. They make great birthday gifts or try mounting one on a journal or album.

Supplies Used:
Aluminum
Alphabet Stencils: Wordsworth
Teflon Embossing Tool
Paper Stump
Black Roller
Decorative Wheels
Acrylic Mat and foam
Ribbon
Cigar Box Lid
Acrylic Paint & Paintbrush
Stamps: PostModern Designs
Silver Ink: Clearsnap
Lightweight Spackle
Crafter's Pick The Ultimate! Adhesive

Cheryl Darrow, Designer

Metal Effects

Transfer image onto metal with embossing tool, emboss and decorate using decorative wheels. (See Basic Instructions.)

Turn metal over and holding the metal in the palm of your hand, puff out the center of the initial with the paper stump. Continue shaping the metal with the paper stump until it has puffed to the height needed.

With the chisel edge Eraser, refine the edges of the initial. This will help the "M" to puff in step #5.

Edge the metal with a decorative wheel. This will give a nice finish to the design.

Flip the metal to the back and holding it in your hand use the paper stump and gently rub back and forth around the "M". Don't rub over the initial as that will flatten it. You want to "puff" the metal around the letter. (Squiggles were added to the front of the metal before this step.)

Turn the metal to the front side and lay flat on the acrylic mat. Using the Black Roller, flatten the edges. This will accentuate the puffed initial. Fill with Spackle and then antique.

Paint the cigar box lid with two different colors of acrylic paint. Let dry. Stamp image on top. Glue on ribbon and apply glue to the back of the letter. Position on top of ribbon.

Metal Effects

Free Form Calligraphy

Cheryl Darrow, Designer

After taking a lettering workshop, I took the practice sheets and embossed some letters on metal for a plaque. These make great gifts for lettering enthusiasts.

Supplies Used:
Pewter
Teflon Embossing Tool
Black Roller
Paper Stump
Cutting Tool
Various Ball & Cups
Oval Wood Plaque: Craft Store
Black Acrylic Paint & Paintbrush
Lightweight Spackle
Crafter's Pick The Ultimate! Glue

Paint a wood plaque with acrylic paint. Hand-letter or use a computer-generated font for the ABC.

Place pewter on the wood plaque and roll with the black roller to define edge.

Emboss the letters on the backside of the metal. Make sure to flip your design before embossing so it's backwards. Decorate the inside of each letter with various decorative wheels and Ball & Cups. Doodle a design around the outside of the letters with the Teflon tip tool.

Metal Effects

Use the puffing process as described on page 29.

Run the cutting tool around the outside edge of the metal and remove excess.

Apply a thin coat of adhesive to the back of the metal and glue to the painted plaque.

....

TIP
Use a 1lb. bag of rice to weigh down the metal to the wood in the gluing stage.
....

Free form calligraphy by Angie Vangalis

This lettering example was written in metal using the medium chisel eraser at a 45° angle. The thick mat must be used beneath the metal sheet to give the letters dimension.

Neuland letter forms by Angie Vangalis

Making block letter forms with the Wide Coarse Dots Decorative Wheel.

Tic Tac Toe

Use individual molds to turn metal into mini works of art. Or why not back with felt and a pin back to create one-of-a-kind jewelry. Make them out of copper to achieve a warmer look.

Supplies Used:
Aluminum
Tic Tac Toe Game Board
Teflon Embossing Tool
Paper Stump
Scissors
Acrylic Mat
Black Acrylic Paint
Mold

Cheryl Darrow, Designer

TIP
Check out craft stores and dollar stores for children's game boards.

Cut metal about 1" larger than the game pieces.

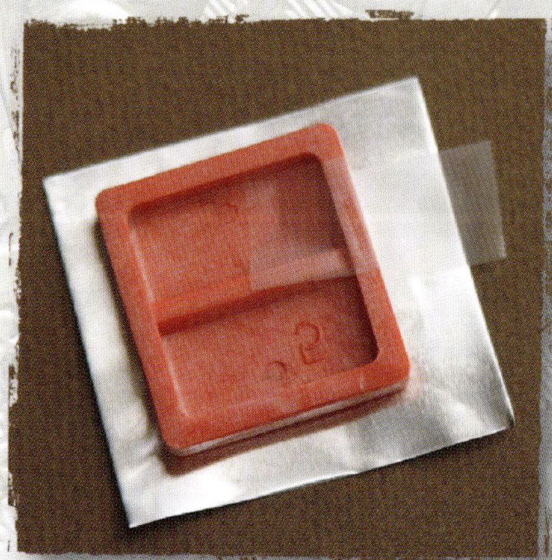

Tape mold to the metal and turn over.

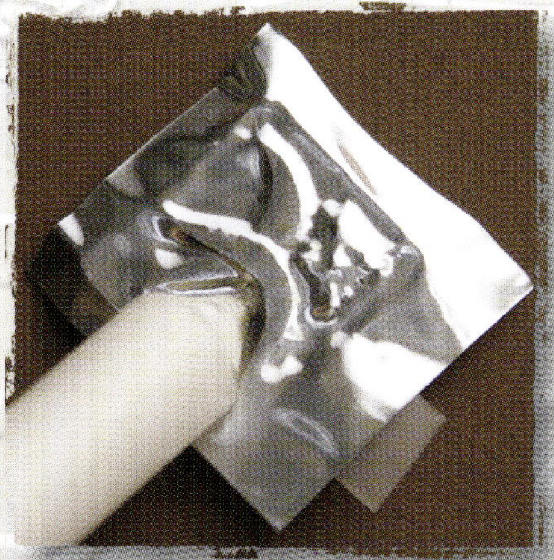

Using the paper stump, rub the top of the metal to create the image from the mold.

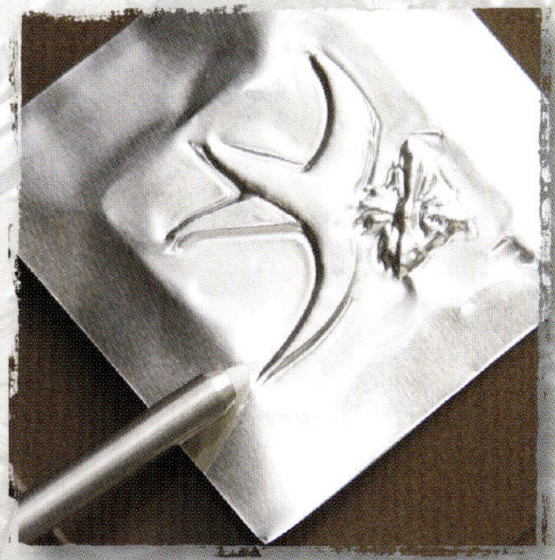

Refine the image with the Teflon embossing tool.

Remove mold and place game piece on the metal. Cut off corners for folding.

Fold metal over the game piece and rub with paper stump to smooth out edges.

TIP
Drill holes in the bottom of the finished piece and add wire and beads.

Metal Effects

Scrapbook Page Projects
Beautiful
YOU WANT BEA ROCK STAR
ROAD TRIP 200
Memories
EVERYONE LOVES UNCLE BOBBY!
Metal Effects

Using Textures & Punches

Cheryl Uribe Designer

Find new uses for plastic templates or even brass stencils. Remember you can use just sections of the templates for your designs.

Supplies Used:
Aluminum
Pattern Paper: K & Co.
Vellum Tag and Eyelet: Making Memories
Silk flowers, Cheesecloth, Ribbon, Beads: Craft Store
Angel sticker: Creative Imaginations
Templates: Francis Meyer, Delta & One Heart…One Mind
Square Punch: Marvy Uchida
Decorative Wheels
Teflon Embossing Tool
Anywhere Hole Punch
Acrylic Paints
Craft Tape
Crafter's Pick The Ultimate! Glue

Cutting metal is a snap when using a large square punch.

Designs on templates take on a new look when embossed on metal. Simply trace the design with the embossing tool and refine edges. Add continuous designs with Decorative Wheels.

Using different acrylic paints, antique the metal and add extra paint around the edges for a shabby chic look. Adhere the squares to the layout with craft tape.

Metal Effects

Memories

For a creative impact on layouts, combine molds, rustic mediums and embellishments to achieve rich texturity.

Supplies Used:
Aluminum
Pattern Paper: Design Originals
Ink Pad: Clearsnap
Brad: Making Memories
Staple, Foam Core, Fun Foam
Rubber Stamps: River City, All Night Media, Image Tree
Ribbon
Tag
Walnut Ink
Charms: The Card Connection
Acrylic Paint
Eyelet: Creative Imagination
Assorted Molds
Teflon Embossing Tool
Paper Stump
Decorative Wheels

Die Cut circle shapes out of Fun Foam and metal.

Place a metal circle on top of foam mat. Trace image through a stencil using the Teflon embossing tool.

Edge circle with Decorative Wheel on foam mat. Glue decorated circle to Fun Foam circle for added dimension.

*T*ape metal to mold. Rub metal using paper stump (as shown on page 22). Refine with Teflon embossing tool.

To support metal, place a piece of foam core on decorated metal as shown above.

To embellish photos, use thin strips of metal that have been debossed with a Decorative Wheel.

TIP

❖ Save scraps of metal to embellish as photo corners.

❖ Add eyelets and brads to give added dimension.

❖ Either side of molded metal can be used.

Metal Effects

Metal & Fibers

Karen Wells, Designer

Page titles take on a special look when made from metal. Metal can be cut with decorative scissors, die cut machines or hole punches.

Supplies Used:
Paper: Basic Grey
Rust Cardstock
Aqua Cardstock
Fibers: Basic Grey
Copper
Copper Brads: Coffee Break Designs
Hole Punch
Black Acrylic Paint
Crafter's Pick The Ultimate! Glue
Teflon Embossing Tool
Decorative Wheels
Ball & Cup

Cut strips of copper metal long enough to fold over fibers and edge with Decorative Wheels.

Emboss or deboss letters on the metal, and add a Ball & Cup.

Fold copper over several lengths of fibers, punch hole through the metal and attach the copper brads. Spread the title over the page and adhere with adhesive behind the metal.

Metal Effects

Metal Frame

Add a touch of elegance to heritage layouts with embossed metal frames.

Supplies used:
Paper: Autumn Leaves
Peach Cardstock
Aluminum
Lightweight Spackle
Black Acrylic Paint
Double-sided Brown Mulberry Paper
Green Ribbon & Charm: Making Memories
Stencil: AlphaBetterTemplates
Computer font: Autumn Leaves-
  Afternoon Delight
Vellum
Xyron Adhesive
Teflon Embossing Tool
Decorative Wheels
Mold #14: Ten Seconds Studio

Karen Wells, Designer

*P*lace metal on top of mold and rub with paper stump.

Refine image with pointed eraser for better detail. Remove metal from mold and refine around image.

Trace name onto the back of metal. Flip metal over and refine around name.

Metal Effects

Hinged Embellishments

Cheryl Uribe, Designer

Incorporating embossed metal letters in scrapbook layouts is a snap when they are die cut.

Supplies Used:
Copper and Black Art Metal
Pattern Paper: Daisy D's & 7 Gypsies
Vellum Tag, Eyelets and Brads: Making Memories
Ribbon, Wire, Staples, Beads, Hinges and Velcro: Craft store
Inkpad: Clearsnap
Stickers: Pebbles Inc., Creative Imaginations
  Deja Views, Doddlebug Designs, EK Success
Dymo Label Maker
Die Cuts: Accu-Cut
Index tab: Avery
Crafter's Pick The Ultimate! Glue
Various Decorative Wheels
Ball & Cup
Teflon Embossing Tool
Square Hole Punch - Marvy Uchida

*C*ut out a piece of metal for the door on the layout. Punch out a square with the square hole punch for the window.

*U*sing the Ball & Cup tool, emboss balls on the back of the door piece.

Flip metal over and use the Cup tool to refine the ball.

Edge the cover with a decorative wheel. Attach vellum tag to front of square punched window.

Add hinges for a unique binding.

Decorated metal is easy to die cut to complement any layout.

TIP

❖ *Die cut embossed metal tape for a fast and easy layout.*

❖ *Incorporate store-bought letters, numbers or stickers with metal.*

Die Cut Letters

This project is a great use for all the decorative templates you have stored away and haven't used in a while.

Supplies Used:
Metals: Copper, Brass, Aluminum and
   Art Metals
Stickers: Me & My Big Ideas, EK Success &
   Sticker Studio
Brads, Eyelets, Chain, Cheesecloth: Craft Stores
Decorative Papers: K & Co.
Dymo Label Maker
Various Die Cuts: Sizzix & Accu-Cut
Templates: Scrap Pagerz, EK Success, Deja
   Views, Making Memories &
   The Crafter's Workshop
Decorative Wheels
Ball & Cups
Teflon Embossing Tool
Acrylic Paint

Cheryl Uribe, Designer

Using Decorative Wheels and Ball & Cups, deboss the designs on the metal.

Select various metals for the different letters. Either cut the designs using die cuts or trace design on the metal with alphabet templates and then cut.

Don't throw away the negative area from the metal strip after it's been die cut. Cut this up and use in your design. As in the "i" in the layout.

Metal Effects

Metal Tape

Karen Wells, Designer

Metal tape is a fast and easy way to add pizazz to any project.

Supplies Used:
Papers: Autumn Leaves
Metal Tape
Craft Knife and Cutting Mat
Craft Tape
Cardstock
Ribbons
Rub-on Letters: Making Memories
Various Decorative Wheels
Teflon Embossing Tool

Cut a strip of metal tape and deboss with the different Decorative Wheels. This is done in a crazy quilt design, which means the decoration covers the entire tape!

Cut the tape into strips as shown on sample.

Layer tape with art strips of patterned papers.

Hand Lettering

Scrapbook pages become special keepsakes when you use your own hand-lettered sayings. Take those same pages to the next level and "emboss" your lettering in metal.

Supplies Used:
Paper: Colorbok, Sonnets
Purple Cardstock
Light Green Cardstock
Aluminum
Lightweight Spackle
Black Acrylic Paint
Handwritten Verbiage on Vellum
Teflon Embossing Tool
Various Decorative Wheels
Various Ball & Cups
Xyron Adhesive
Crafter's Pick The Ultimate! Glue

TIP
Add Spackle to the back of the metal saying and wipe off excess. This will keep the lettering from being crushed.

Karen Wells, Designer

***H**andwrite or computer-generate the saying on vellum. Turn the vellum over and on the backside of the metal emboss the saying backwards. Antique.*

Emboss and deboss a piece of metal for the "tie back" on the layout.

Metal Effects

Gallery

Debossed Frame
Cheryl Uribe

Stencil Emblem
Cheryl Uribe

Word Strips
Karen Wells

Letter Die Cuts
Cheryl Uribe

Metal Effects

Gallery

Grapevine　　　　*Cheryl Uribe*

Art Metal Kisses　　　　*Cheryl Uribe*

Way 2 Cute　　　　*Cheryl Uribe*

Metal Effects

Bathing Beauty　　　　*Cheryl Uribe*

Gallery

Keepsake Box   Lisa Hoffman

"Beaded Wall Art"   Cheryl Darrow

Wooden Apples   Angie Vangalis

Soda Can Art   Cheryl Darrow

Metal Effects

Gallery

Copper Tile Art   *Karen Wells*

Album Cover   *Cheryl Darrow*

Torched Copper   *Angie Vangalis*

Journal Cover   *Cheryl Darrow*

Metal Effects

48

Resources

3 Ring Circles
www.3ringcircles.com

7Gypsies
www.7gypsies.com

Accent
(800) fine art

Accu-Cut
www.accucut.com

All Night Media
See Plaid Enterprises

Amaco
www.amaco.com

Ampersand Art Supply
www.ampersandart.com

Anita's Paints
"Back Street Inc. Dublin, GA"

Apple Barrel
(800) fine art

Art Accents Inc.
See Provo Craft

Artistic Wire
(630) 530-7567

Autumn Leaves
www.autumnleaves.com

Avery Dennison
www.averydennison.com

Basic Grey
www.basicgrey.com

Bazzill Basics Paper
www.bazzillbasics.com

Card Connection
Available at Michaels.com

Chatterbox Inc.
www.chatterboxinc.com

Clearsnap/Colorbox
www.clearsnap.com

Coffee Break Designs
(317)-290-1542

Colorbok
www.colorbok.com

Crafter's Pick
www.crafterspick.com

Crafter's Workshop
www.thecraftersworkshop.com

Crafts Etc.
www.craftsetc.com

Creative Imaginations
www.cigift.com

Crystall Ball
Available at Dollartree stores

Daisy D's Paper
www.daisydspaper.com

Dayco
www.daycodiecuts.com

Delta
www.deltacrafts.com

Deja Views

C-thru ruler
(860) 243-0303

DeNami Design
(253) 437-1626

Design Press
www.designpress.com

Die Cuts with a View
www.diecutswithaview.com

Doodlebug Designs
www.doodlebugdesigninc.com

Dymo
www.dymo.com

EK Success
www.eksuccess.com

Family Treasures
www.familytreasures.com

Francis Meyer Inc.
www.francesmeyer.com

Hero Arts
www.heroarts.com

Hobby Lobby
www.hobbylobby.com

Image Tree
See EK Success

K & Co.
www.kandcompany.com

KI Memories
www.kimemories.com

Lion Brand Yarn
www.lionbrand.com

Magenta
www.magentastyle.com

Magic Mesh
www.magicmesh.com

Magic Scraps
www.magicscraps.com

Making Memories
www.makingmemories.com

Marvy Uchida
www.uchida.com

Me & My Big Ideas
www.meandmybigideas.com

Michaels Craft Stores
www.michaels.com

Offray
www.offray.com

Once Upon a Scribble
www.onceuponascribble.com

One heart...One mind
Available at www.stuff4scrapbooking.com

Plaid Enterprises
www.plaidonline.com

PostModern Designs
(405) 321-3176

Pebbles Inc.
www.pebblesinc.com

Provo Craft
www.provocraft.com

River City Rubber Works
www.rivercityrubberworks.com

Rubber Stampede
www.rubberstampede.com

Scrap Pagerz
www.scrappagerz.com

Sizzix
www.sizzix.com

Sten Source
www.craftworksrp.com

Sticker Studio
www.stickerstudio.com

"Tsukineko, Inc."
www.tsukineko.com

Twelve Timbers
www.traylorpapers.com

Walnut Hallow
www.walnuthallow.com

Wordsworth Art Stamps
www.wordsworthstamps.com

Xyron
www.xyron.com

....

Contributing Artists

Ten Seconds Studio
www.tensecondsstudio.com

Hoffman, Lisa
lisahoffman@qwest.net

Uribe, Cheryl
cusmile.biz@verizon.net

Vangalis, Angie
angie@avgraphics.net

Wells, Karen
hideko32@aol.com

Copper Sampler Album

Copper Embossed Cover for Scrapbook

Cheryl Darrow